P9-DER-545

Oh, Wow!

THE MINIATURE QUILTS & THEIR MAKERS

MAQS

Oh, Wow!

THE MINIATURE QUILTS & THEIR MAKERS

AT THE MUSEUM OF THE AMERICAN QUILTER'S SOCIETY

Oh Wow: the Miniature Quilts and Their Makers at the Museum of the American Quilter's Society

American Quilter's Society
P.O. Box 3290
Paducah, KY 42002-3290

Located in Paducah, Kentucky, the American Quilter's Society (AQS) is dedicated to promoting the accomplishments of today's quilters. Through its publications and events, AQS strives to honor today's quiltmakers and their work and to inspire future creativity and innovation in quiltmaking.

Editor: Editors of the American Quilter's Society
Graphic Design: Amy Chase
Cover Design: Michael Buckingham
Photography: Charles R. Lynch

Library of Congress Cataloging-in-Publication Data
American Quilter's Society.
    Oh wow; the miniature quilts and their makers at the Museum of the American Quilter's Society. / American Quilter's Society.
        p. cm.
Summary: "Collection of miniature quilts of the Oh, Wow! Collection at the Museum of the American Quilter's Society. The miniature quilts contain all the detail and complexity of the full-sized quilts, yet are done to scale in a 24" x 24" or smaller format. Collection features best-known and frequently honored quiltmakers" -- Provided by publisher.
        Includes bibliographical references and index.
        ISBN 978-1-57432-931-5 (alk. paper) – ISBN 978-1-57432-930-8 (leatherbound ed.)
        1. Miniature quilts--United States--Catalogs. 2. Miniature quilts--Kentucky--Paducah--Catalogs. 3. MAQS--Catalogs. I. Title.

NK9112.A539 2007
746.460973'07476995--dc22
                2007002614

Additional copies of this book may be ordered from the American Quilter's Society, PO Box 3290, Paducah, KY 42002-3290; 800-626-5420 (orders only please); or online at www.AmericanQuilter.com. For all other inquiries, please call 270-898-7903.

Copyright © 2007, American Quilter's Society

All rights reserved. No part of this book may be reproduced, stored in any retrieval system, or transmitted in any form, or by any means including but not limited to electronic, mechanical, photocopy, recording, or otherwise without the written consent of the author and publisher.

On the cover: PINEAPPLE SURPRISE by Judy Spiers

Dedication

In appreciation of the makers of outstanding
Oh, Wow! miniature quilts—past, present, and future

In recognition of the talent and needle skills necessary
to create small-scale replicas of traditional and contemporary quilts

*Books are not judged by their covers
nor masterpiece quilts by their size.*

Contents

Introduction

In 1995, miniature quilts were added to the list of competition categories at the AQS Quilt Show and Contest in Paducah, Kentucky. The glass covered cases that showcased these tiny works of art were in close proximity to the show entrance where, for 20 plus years, I have greeted the public.

Occasionally, I would walk over to the miniature display, and more often than not, I would hear someone say, "Oh, wow! Look at that one" or "Oh, wow! Can you believe that?" Sometimes, due to a loss of words, I simply heard, "Oh, wow!" I quickly became a fan of miniature quilts and their makers, reveling at their artistic abilities. I found I was spending as much time admiring the miniatures at the cases as I was at the entrance to the show.

When my wife, Meredith, came to me asking if I had an idea for a plan to raise monies for the Museum of the American Quilter's Society's (MAQS) Acquisition Fund, it was only natural for me to think of miniatures. After giving it some thought, I decided that a collection of miniature quilts to be displayed at the museum with a book featuring those quilts and their makers would be the perfect solution. All proceeds from the book would go to the MAQS Acquisition Fund.

I personally contacted as many quiltmakers as I thought could make a "to-scale" miniature quilt. The response I received was overwhelming. The 42-quilt collection is simply, Oh, wow!

From the beginning, Selim Benardete, founder and president emeritus of Benartex, now a division of Bernina of America, has sponsored the miniature category at the AQS Quilt Show and Contest. Due to his participation and sponsorship over the years, the president of Benartex, David Lochner, suggested that AQS and MAQS honor Selim by showcasing his name on the plaque that accompanies the collection both while traveling and on exhibit at the museum.

There are two different bindings of this book: a standard casebound edition as well as a special, numbered limited edition in bonded leather. Those who generously donate a minimum of five hundred dollars to the Museum of the American Quilters Society will receive the special edition, limited to only 250 copies.

It is my intention to continue to add quilts to this collection and add a second *Oh, Wow!* book in the next couple of years. This will perpetuate this important fund for quiltmakers and quilt lovers across the globe.

My thanks to Klaudeen Hansen of Sun Prairie, Wisconsin, for her invaluable help in assembling this collection.

Bill Schroeder
Co-Founder
Museum of the American Quilter's Society

Teri Barile

ARTIST'S STATEMENT

Having my quilt invited to become part of the museum collection is a dream come true. I love attention to detail and although it is fun on a big quilt, it is a real challenge to me in a miniature. I feel such a sense of accomplishment when I finish a miniature quilt because of the time and effort it has taken and the challenge it has presented to me. The patience it takes to piece a miniature block has greatly improved my piecing in standard quilts. Because the quilt THERE AND BACK AGAIN gets its title from the book *Lord of the Rings*, it explains the journey my heart, soul, and hands went through while completing this quilt.

BIO

Quilting since she was old enough to hold a needle and piecing her first block at the age of nine or ten, Teri did not begin to make miniature quilts until 2004. At the urging of a guild member, a small group, The Twisted Stitchers, was formed and Teri's passion for making miniature quilts was initiated. Teri began entering competitions in 2005 for the drive it gives her to create and do her best work. THERE AND BACK AGAIN was juried into the 2006 AQS Quilt Show and Contest and received an honorable mention in the 2006 NQA Show. This is only the second quilt Teri has entered into competition and the second miniature she has completed.

> QUILT DESCRIPTION

THERE AND BACK AGAIN was designed after taking an online class at Quilt University with Jane Hall. The Pineapples Plus class was the inspiration for this miniature using the color placement technique. The quilt was planned on graph paper and finished in EQ5 with eighteen different color gradations and up to five color changes in each block. Straight line quilting was chosen to create a secondary star design.

THERE AND BACK AGAIN

14" x 14"

Bonnie K. Browning

ARTIST'S STATEMENT

The mid-nineteenth century Baltimore-style quilts have always intrigued me. They have incredible detail and are usually set together in an album of blocks. I enjoy embroidery and decided that if I were ever going to complete a Baltimore Album style quilt, it would be stitched with silk ribbon. And so, this being my inspiration, I set about designing blocks that would exemplify this method.

BIO

Bonnie Browning started her career in quilting in the 1970s when she made her first quilt top in a Welcome Wagon group. From there, she began teaching quilt classes for the local art center. In 1986, Bonnie received certification as a quilt judge from the National Quilting Association and put together a list of different classes in order to teach and judge at quilt shows. Currently, she is the executive show director for the American Quilter's Society. Initiating the Quilt Camp for Kids at the Museum of the American Quilter's Society, serving as technical consultant for *American Quilter,* and appearing on multiple quilting shows are all part of Bonnie's résumé. She is also the author of nine quilting books.

QUILT DESCRIPTION

SMITTEN WITH FLOWERS uses variegated silk ribbon to give the quilt more dimension. The designs are stitched onto a single piece of cotton fabric, with cable stitching on the outline and border. Hundreds of colonial knots make up the clusters of grapes, with dimension created by understitching with straight stitches. A ¼-inch grid is quilted for the background and a cable that mimics the shape of the stitched ribbon border is quilted in the outside border.

SMITTEN WITH FLOWERS
14½" x 14½"

Judith Day

ARTIST'S STATEMENT

I made DANCING AT NETHERFIELD specifically for the 1997 AQS Quilt Show and Contest where it won first place in the miniature category. I thoroughly enjoyed making the dancing doll border as I tried to capture the essence of English Country dance in the early nineteenth century. Just as they did in Charles Bingley's ballroom at Netherfield in Jane Austen's novel *Pride and Prejudice*, here, eager young ladies in their beautiful dresses line up to flirt their way into the hearts of dashing young gentlemen. This quilt is my favorite miniature as it was an absolute joy to make.

BIO

With a lifelong passion for sewing, Judith Day grew up sewing and knitting in Sydney, Australia. Before entering school, she was able to crochet and knit. By the age of 10, Judy won her first prize in appliqué for a Mexican man buttonhole stitched onto a green laundry bag. In 1985, her quilting adventure began when she learned to do Cathedral Window patchwork. Miniature quilts became part of her obsession in 1989 after entering an Amish Miniature Challenge. Since 1995, Judy's miniature quilts have won nine different times in the AQS Miniature category. She has also won many awards at the Sydney Quilt Show and the Festival of Quilts in England.

> QUILT DESCRIPTION

DANCING AT NETHERFIELD was inspired by a photo of a nineteenth-century quilt owned by the National Trust of South Australia. The hexagons were made over paper using the English method. The whole quilt was appliquéd onto a square of muslin. This quilt was created starting first with the borders, working inwards to the center of the quilt. The center design features a *broderie perse* bouquet cut from a piece of Liberty lawn purchased in London.

DANCING AT NETHERFIELD

22¼" x 22½"

Judith Day

ARTIST'S STATEMENT

FLOWER POT IN A COTTAGE GARDEN was made for the
2000 AQS Quilt Show and Contest where it won
second place in the miniature category. It took home
a first place as a traditional wallhanging at Sydney's
Royal Easter show in 2001. I started the miniature
in July of 1999 and it took a mere four months to
complete. As I worked on it, I imagined that the
flower pot was sitting in a cottage garden of beautiful
flowers and climbing roses, hence the title.

> QUILT DESCRIPTION

FLOWER POT IN A COTTAGE GARDEN was created
using one of Florence Peto's quilts as an
inspiration. The whole design was drawn onto
a piece of cream muslin with a blue washable
pen. Needleturn appliqué was then employed
using the pen lines as a guide. This quilt was
made using a number of tiny scraps and mail
order samples. The quilting and stippling
accentuate the appliqué.

FLOWER POT IN A COTTAGE GARDEN

15" x 20½"

Caryl Bryer Fallert

ARTIST'S STATEMENT

For as long as I can remember, I have expressed myself through artwork. Although my formal training was primarily in design, drawing, and studio painting, I discovered that fabric, as an artistic medium, best expressed my personal vision. I love the tactile qualities of cloth and the unlimited color range made possible by hand dyeing. The focus of my work is on the qualities of color, line, and texture, which will engage the spirit and emotions of the viewer. I intend for my quilts to be seen and enjoyed by others. It is my hope that they will lift the spirits and delight the eyes of those who see them.

BIO

For the past twenty-three years, Caryl Bryer Fallert's work has been exhibited extensively throughout North America, Europe, Japan, and the Pacific Rim. Caryl's attention to detail has earned her a reputation for fine craftsmanship and stunning design. In 2000, Caryl was selected as one of the thirty most influential quiltmakers in the world. The recipient of the Bernina Leadership Award in 2003 and voted as an AQS All-American Quilter in 2004, she is the only three-time winner of the Best of Show Award from American Quilter's Society. Her quilts have received Best of Show honors in fifteen other national and international exhibitions. Caryl is the 2006 recipient of the International Quilt Festival Silver Star Award.

> QUILT DESCRIPTION

MIDNIGHT FANTASY #8 was based on a digital photograph of the unquilted top of award-winning quilt MIDNIGHT FANTASY #6. The image was altered so that the miniature is not an exact replica of the full-size design. Digital manipulation was done in Corel Draw® and the image was printed on an ink-jet printer. It was machine quilted, taking the same amount of time to quilt as the original large quilt.

MIDNIGHT FANTASY #8

12½" x 18¼"

Sherry Fourez

ARTIST'S STATEMENT

From my first time at the AQS Quilt Show, I dreamed about having a quilt accepted. If I didn't win a ribbon, I would still be proud that my quilt was there hanging among all the other beautiful quilts. I decided to make this Pineapple quilt for the miniature category. This quilt was made with only two fabrics: the black and the stripe. That was an accomplishment in itself. When Bill Schroeder asked if I would donate this quilt to the MAQS collection, I was ecstatic and emphatically said yes. Having my quilt displayed with this collection is better than winning a ribbon, as it will be available for quilters to see in the future.

BIO

Sherry Fourez did not begin making miniature quilts until she returned home from the 2005 AQS Quilt Show and Contest in Paducah, Kentucky. By April of 2006, she had already completed 20 miniature quilts and had one juried into the 2006 AQS Quilt Show and Contest. Although making miniatures is a relatively new adventure for Sherry, her passion for quiltmaking is longstanding. Her quilting career began by taking a class at a local church and has since greatly expanded. A competitive quilter, she had quilts juried into both Paducah and Nashville in 2006. Sherry is also a quilt teacher and lecturer.

> QUILT DESCRIPTION

SPARKLING PINEAPPLE MINI QUILT was based on the Pineapple block designed by Cindi Edgerton of a Very Special Collection. Made using only two different fabrics, the fabrics were cut apart into strips, arranged from lights to darks, and then sewn into the pineapple pattern. The entire quilt is made of 25 blocks totaling 1,125 pieces. The blocks were foundation pieced and machine quilted. Four hundred eighty-four Swarovski® crystals were then added to display a secondary pattern.

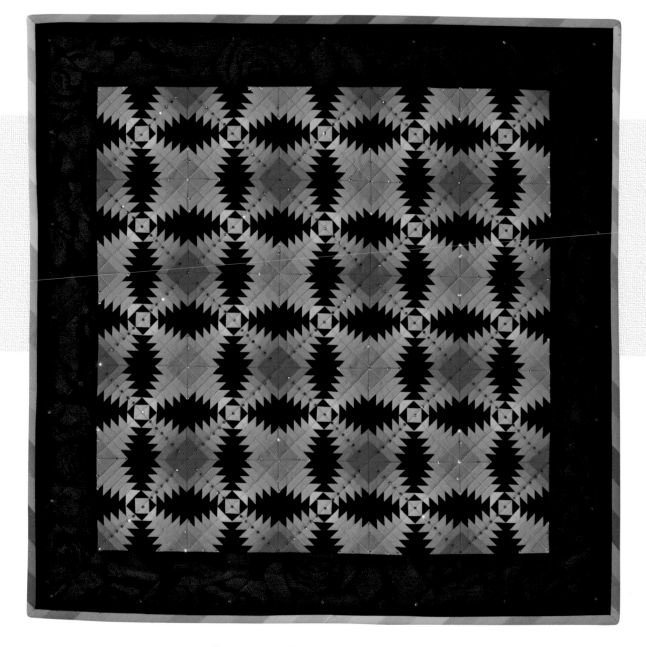

SPARKLING PINEAPPLE MINI QUILT

24" x 24"

Diane Gaudynski

ARTIST'S STATEMENT

A pleasure to quilt, this original miniature design is similar to vintage wholecloth quilts. The mood of it, the elegance and formality, the details and designs, the sheer joyfulness of it all are a reflection of these old quilts, but done with modern techniques. I let the designs go where they seemed to belong, to balance space, to create movement, harmony, and excitement in the design itself. Quilting this was a marvelous challenge to me, and when finished, I felt as if it had almost quilted itself. I was only the onlooker as each design unfolded in front of me.

BIO

A self-taught quilter, Diane Gaudynski began machine quilting in 1988 using Harriet Hargrave's first book as her guide. In 2001, she was named one of the Top Thirty Quilters of the World. By the year 2002, she was awarded the title Master Quilter by the National Quilting Association. Considered to be an accomplished designer, many of her quilts are showcased in museums and private collections. Diane has authored two books as well as numerous articles in quilting magazines. A Wisconsin native, she is known for her ornate original quilting designs and her subtle and sophisticated use of "mud" colors. Many of her quilts have won top awards at AQS, NQA, and other national quilt shows.

> QUILT DESCRIPTION

A VISIT TO PROVENCE is an original design miniature wholecloth quilt. The inspiration came from books that contained vintage Provence quilts. After scouring the pages for design elements that would suit a miniature theme, the designs were mapped out in basic areas to be quilted. The feather groups in the border were quilted freehand with no drawing. The tiny freehand circles, like a string of pearls, are based on the same motifs in the original quilts.

A VISIT TO PROVENCE

23" x 24"

Jane Hall

ARTIST'S STATEMENT

I am intrigued by the interactions of colors in fabrics and the graphics of quilt designs, especially the geometry of Log Cabin and Pineapple patterns. My work is usually based on traditional forms of quiltmaking, using contemporary techniques and innovative sets and colorations to create something new, often with subtle but recognizable form. I have a particular interest in foundations, and in exploring and teaching ways of using them in all kinds of piecing—traditional to innovative. I feel that miniature quilts are a wonderful way to have the "punch" of a full-sized quilt in a limited space.

BIO

Jane Hall has lectured and taught quiltmaking for guilds and quilt conferences in the United States and abroad for more than twenty years. She is a certified teacher, judge, and appraiser for antique and contemporary quilts. Her award-winning quilts have been exhibited nationally and internationally and are included in public and private collections. Author and coauthor (with Dixie Haywood) of several books on different aspects of foundation work, Jane's primary interest is foundation design and piecing, traditional and innovative, with particular emphasis on Pineapples.

> QUILT DESCRIPTION

INDIGO LIGHTS II was made in 2006 specifically to participate in the miniature quilt project for the Museum of the American Quilter's Society. It is a small scale version of INDIGO LIGHTS, also made by Jane Hall. Batik prints, hand-dyed fabric, and beige calicoes were the fabrics of choice. The design of the quilt was inspired by an antique silk quilt in the Shelburne Museum, using a block with both Log Cabin and Pineapple elements.

INDIGO LIGHTS II

12½" X 12½"

Klaudeen Hansen

ARTIST'S STATEMENT

An enduring interest in Amish style quilts led me to make over twenty-five different pieced variations. This one is the smallest and therefore appropriate to donate to the Oh, Wow! collection. My interest in the Amish quilts continues as my plan includes piecing small versions of the other three Amish quilt postage stamps from the year 2000.

BIO

Teaching quiltmaking and judging quilts are two of Klaudeen Hansen's favorite activities. An extremely active teacher, she currently teaches nationally and internationally for guilds and conferences. When she isn't judging quilt contests herself, she enjoys training future judges. As competition chairperson of the AQS Quilt Show & Contest, quiltmaking still consumes much of her time. Klaudeen is the coeditor of the yearly *Quilt Art Engagement Calendar,* author of *Addresses & Birthdays,* and she also earned a spot in *Who's Who in American Quilting.* Her Amish quilts have been exhibited all over the United States, Europe, and Japan.

> QUILT DESCRIPTION

AMISH STAMP QUILT was inspired by the 2000 United States postage stamp. The pattern is known by the Amish as Diamond in a Square. This miniature was machine pieced and hand quilted by Klaudeen Hansen and Arlene Statz. The hand quilting showcases differences in the quilting stitch, which is typical of full-size Amish made quilts.

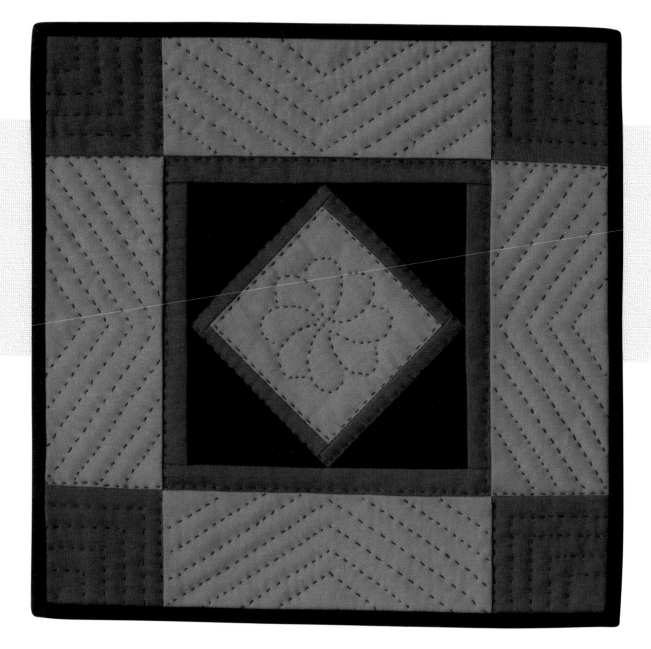

AMISH STAMP QUILT

8½" x 8½"

Jessie Harrison

ARTIST'S STATEMENT

Let me start by saying I love miniatures—all kinds of miniatures. The first mini quilts I made were a definite learning process. Not only did they have very small pieces, but they had to be made to scale. The first quilts I made were traditional quilts pieced to scale. This is when I learned the value of the glue stick. With a glue stick, very small pieces can be held in place and sewn with precision. As time goes on, my quilts get bigger. But no matter how big my quilts get, I still have that first thought when I see an interesting pattern: "I wonder how small I can make that…"*

*Note: The artist's statement was taken from an article in the Winter 2001 issue of the *American Quilter* magazine.

BIO

It wasn't until after her children were in high school and she finished her education that Jessie Harrison entered the workforce as a computer specialist in the aerospace industry. When she entered a shop that sold miniature doll houses in 1990, she felt like she was entering a fairyland. After completing a doll house and a miniature doll, Jessie began to make pillows, rugs, doilies, and knitted sweaters for the doll. She was so enthused she began a miniatures business in 1991. Realizing that she could make miniature quilts for her doll, Jessie found her new passion. Her work has appeared in numerous publications and received countless awards. Jessie left a great legacy in the quilting world when she passed away in 2002.

> QUILT DESCRIPTION

THE BOUQUET is an original design miniature quilt. Techniques such as mini-applique, 3-D flowers, trapunto, and quilting are exemplified in this quilt. The stylized butterflies in the corners contribute to the overall beauty. The quilt was hand appliquéd and hand quilted. It won two first-place awards as well as the Outstanding Mini award from the 2001 Road to California show.

Jessie Harrison

THE BOUQUET

9¾" x 11¾"

Jessie Harrison

> ## QUILT DESCRIPTION

BLOSSOMS AND BERRIES was created using Hoffman Bali fabrics. The hand appliqué was done using silk thread. Hand quilting enhances this miniature. It received a first-place award in the 2001 IQA show in Houston, Texas, as well as the 2002 AQS Quilt Show in Paducah, Kentucky. In 2002, the quilt received Outstanding Mini at Road to California.

BLOSSOMS AND BERRIES

$10\frac{7}{8}"$ x $10\frac{7}{8}"$

Jane Holihan

ARTIST'S STATEMENT

Antique quilts have always been my favorite, and the bright contrast of the red-and-green quilts especially caught my eye. I took on the challenge of designing one in the miniature style, responding to my admiration for these small treasures. I have discovered that alternating my miniature and large quilt projects brings great satisfaction. Workmanship and hand quilting are the most important parts of my quilting. Finishing a quilt by hand is extemely rewarding, and improving and trying to better each quilt I make is always my goal.

BIO

A quilter since the mid 1970s, Jane Holihan has won numerous awards. In her quilting career, her quilts have received 106 first-place, 18 second-place, and 12 third-place ribbons; 30 awards for fine workmanship; and 39 Best of Show awards. These awe-inspiring quilts have been featured in magazines, exhibited in museums, and shown as part of special invitations. Jane Holihan has also been the featured artist in several exhibits. She was named a Master Quilter in 1997, when her quilt was awarded the prestigious Master Quilt Award. In 2000, she received the AQS Quilt Exposition Grand Prize Award.

> QUILT DESCRIPTION

PRIMROSE features an original appliqué design with detailed quilting patterns. It was embellished with a touch of embroidery and trapunto to accentuate the quilting designs. Hand quilted, PRIMROSE was completed in three months. The major winnings for this quilt include eight first-place ribbons in national and international shows, as well as a Best of Show Miniature award.

Jane Holihan

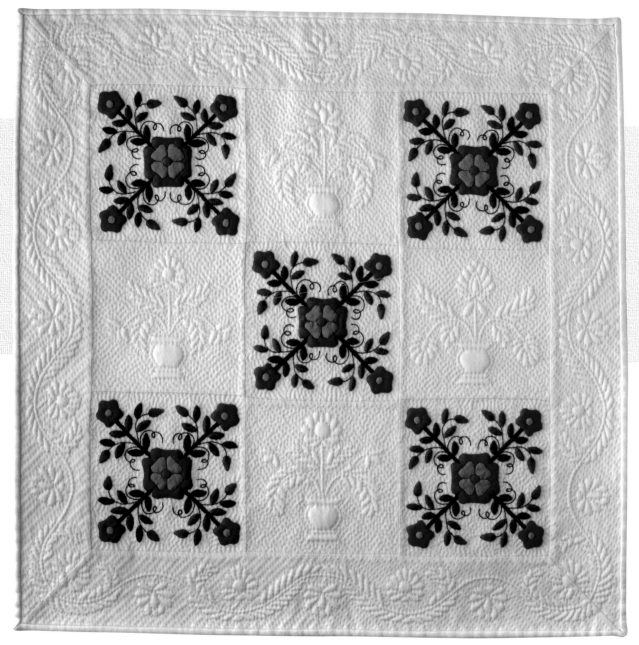

PRIMROSE

15½" x 15½"

Jane Holihan

ARTIST'S STATEMENT

I am enthralled with antique quilts and their traditional beauty. Since my other love is for nature, I feel it only fitting that I include both in my quilts. I have learned the most over the years through experience, speaking with others, and with much practice. Quilting lets me express in fabric that which I cannot accomplish in painting. It gives me great pleasure to be able to design what nature inspires, and then to see my patterns and quilting designs come to life in a finished quilt.

> QUILT DESCRIPTION

The initial inspiration for ROSE SPLENDOR came from a simple bird. The urn and the flowers were designed as a resting place for the bird. Tiny butterflies and silk embroidery finished the quilt top. The needle-turn appliqué was done by hand using the freezer-paper method. Hand quilting and trapunto were used to bring the quilt to life. This quilt was entered into three international shows and received three first-place ribbons.

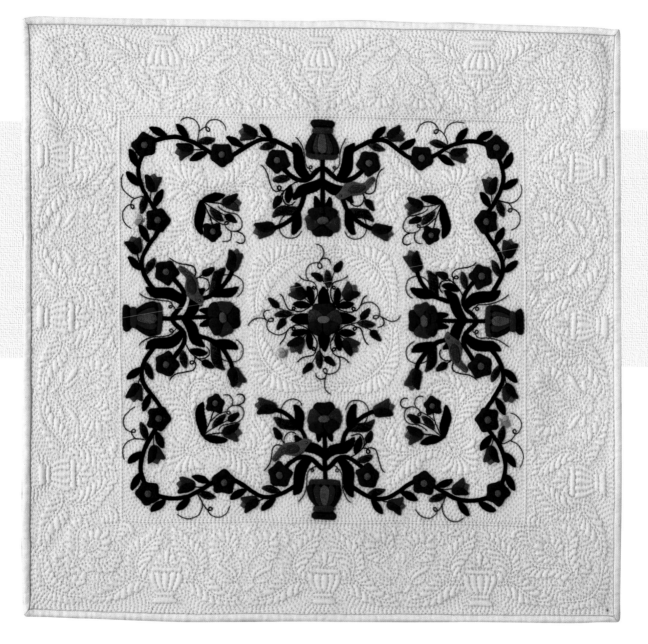

ROSE SPLENDOR

17" x 17"

Pat Holly

ARTIST'S STATEMENT

I have always been fascinated with miniature textiles. When I first learned to knit, I began making tiny sweaters and dresses for my Barbie® dolls. The passion for small things has stayed with me and I now enjoy creating miniature quilts. The inspiration for my quilts is drawn from many avenues. Regardless of the inspiration, it is the technique that is an essential part of my work. As I watched my mother machine sew from a young age, it was natural for me to turn to machine techniques when I discovered quiltmaking. Designing and stitching tiny quilts are both a joy and a challenge to me. I plan to continue making, sharing, and teaching others what I love to do.

BIO

Author, teacher, and quiltmaker, Pat Holly has been quilting for over twenty years and entering competitions for the last ten. She attended the University of Michigan School of Art studying color, graphic design, weaving, and fabric design. THE SPACE QUILT, made with her sister Sue Nickels, won the Bernina Machine Quilting award at the 2004 AQS Quilt Show and Contest. It was at this same show that the miniature FIFTY BIRDS won 3rd prize in the miniature category. In 2006, Pat and Sue coauthored the book *Stitched Raw Edge Applique*.

> QUILT DESCRIPTION

FIFTY BIRDS developed from the inspiration of Pat's 50th birthday as well as an antique quilt that was covered in simple birds. Those two themes were incorporated to make up the central focus of the quilt, while a small pieced border as well as a border for quilting were added to make the overall design look like a complete quilt. A tiny piping and stitched details were combined in the binding, adding more interest to the birds.

FIFTY BIRDS

12" x 14"

Charlotte Huber

ARTIST'S STATEMENT

When I realized that my quilts had traveled to far more places than I ever had, I decided I should travel across the country as well. So, when my husband retired, we began our journey stopping at every town with a quilt shop. I love to talk to the shop owners about the history of the area and purchase something in every store. I always remember where my design ideas come from and what part of the country inspired me. I believe that my quilts are truly American works of art.

BIO

Charlotte Huber's love for sewing began at a very young age when she learned to hand sew. Only when she was able to reach the treadle on her grandmother's sewing machine did she learn the art of machine sewing. In 1972, she won a quilt in a church raffle and it was then that her fascination for quilting came full circle. Her quilts have won many awards in local and regional shows as well as throughout the country. Charlotte has also been published in several magazines.

> QUILT DESCRIPTION

HAWAIIAN HOLIDAY is based on an original design called JUBILEE ALBUM, created for Fons & Porter's *Love of Quilting* magazine by designers Sue Nickels and Pat Holly. The original quilt ran as a series beginning with the March/April 2003 issue and concluding with March/April 2004 issue. Charlotte adapted the design to make a miniature quilt to enter in a miniature quilt contest sponsored by *Love of Quilting*. Entrants had to adapt a pattern from the magazine in order to enter. HAWAIIAN HOLIDAY was the first place winner in the contest. Used with permmission.

HAWAIIAN HOLIDAY
18½" x 18½"

Susan Jackson

ARTIST'S STATEMENT

After recovering from two different surgeries, I decided to pull out some of the fabric scraps from a large quilt I had been working on. Adding some new fabric, and discarding some of the old, I was ready to make BLACK-EYED SUSAN. I made the quilt to please myself and no one else. It was my way of healing both mentally and physically. I didn't intend to enter the quilt into competition, but decided to when I found out it met the specifications for both Road to California and the AQS show. Although it did not receive a ribbon at AQS, I decided to donate the miniature for the Oh, Wow! project.

BIO

Although she never took a class in home economics or majored in art or design, Susan Jackson has always had a sewing machine close by. While trained in business, mechanical engineering, and architecture, it is quilting and her "Susie Homemaker" duties that give her the most gratification.

> QUILT DESCRIPTION

BLACK-EYED SUSAN was computer drafted from scratch. The fan units were paper pieced from scraps and new fabrics to create a full spectrum of light, medium, and dark values against a deep saturated red. Using homemade templates, the curved edges were appliquéd in place. The black-eyed Susans were free-motion stitched for exactness. The miniature was machine quilted.

BLACK-EYED SUSAN

19¼" x 22"

Helen Higginbottom Jacobson

ARTIST'S STATEMENT

The first question in my mind when I think of a quilt is, "How small can I make it?" PRIMROSE LANE was a group challenge to make a full-size quilt. I made the full-size version, but at the same time, I made the quilt in miniature scale. At the guild's reveal meeting, I had both quilts. They were both exhibited in the 2005 AQS Quilt Show and Contest. It was from there that the miniature was invited into the Oh, Wow! collection. Making miniature quilts fulfills my creative needs and grants me the challenge I enjoy.

BIO

In 1982, Helen Higginbottom Jacobson took a class on making quilts and was hooked. As her quiltmaking skills progressed, she found greater joy in the challenge of making a miniature quilt. It was hostessing for Sew Great Tours that sparked her interest in entering the AQS Quilt Show and Contest in Paducah, Kentucky. Since then, she has had five quilts displayed in that show. She is a member of the American Quilter's Society, the International Quilt Association, the Iowa Quilter's Guild, and Just Friends Quilting.

> QUILT DESCRIPTION

MINIATURE PRIMROSE LANE was adapted from the Primrose Lane Quilt pattern by Elaine A. Waldschmitt of the Quilted Closet, Inc. It consists of small Flying Geese, Log Cabin blocks, Star blocks and an appliquéd border. A large Flying Geese design surrounds the center medallion. The quilt is machine appliquéd, machine pieced, and machine quilted. It was awarded a blue ribbon at the Iowa State Fair in 2004 and the Iowa Quilter's Guild Show in 2005.

Helen Higginbottom Jacobson

MINIATURE PRIMROSE LANE

18" x 22"

Shirley P. Kelly

ARTIST'S STATEMENT

After reflecting on a question asked by Bill Schroeder if I made miniature quilts, I realized that I had worked with miniature pieces in conjunction with my usual gigantic quilts. Normally, I used small components to help convey the basic theme. I decided that making a small quilt would be a fun, relaxing respite from my current large quilt. How long could it possibly take? I figured a few hours work for a couple of weeks. Little did I know that this fun project would be a learning experience of solving countless problems. It was a great accomplishment to complete this quilt, but believe me it was pure joy to get back to my usual large quilts.

BIO

Shirley P. Kelly is an award-winning quilter known for her quilts portraying animals, especially horses. While her work as a high school art instructor had given her much experience in working with small-scale projects, CIGAR, IN FRONT was the first miniature quilt she ever attempted. Her large quilts have won her many Best of Show awards, an AQS Machine Workmanship award, a Best Wall Quilt Award, and the title of Master Quilter from NQA in 2005.

> QUILT DESCRIPTION

CIGAR, IN FRONT is an appliquéd piece that was assembled using starched fabric templates as a foundation that could be left in place during the appliqué process. Developed over two months and worked on for seven days a week and fourteen hours a day, this miniature quilt was quite the learning experience for the creator.

CIGAR, IN FRONT

14¾" x 21¼"

June Kempston

Artist's Statement

Every quilt has a story. It may have been stitched with love for a special person or occasion, or it could stand for memories of people, events, or places that are a part of its making. It may be an untold story—special only to the quilter. I feel a quilt's name is an important part of the story. After much consideration, a name will finally fit the quilt. My greatest joy and honor came in being the mother to my son, Jason, whose life came to an end at the young age of 23. IDLEWOOD ROSE was the only quilt he called by a different name: ROSE OF MAMALOU. To honor Jason, I share this quilt, his life and love.

Bio

June Kempston was self-taught in the art of sewing, but her interest turned to quilting around thirty years ago. A traditional quilter, she noticed that the pieces in her quilts grew smaller as her son grew older. Thus, miniature quiltmaking became her passion. Her work includes machine piecing as well as hand appliqué. Many of June's quilts have been exhibited and received honors throughout the country.

Quilt Description

IDLEWOOD ROSE was inspired by the full-size quilt CHESAPEAKE ROSE from the book *Quilts from the Smithsonian* by Mimi Dietrich. The hand appliqué was done using the needle-turn technique with freezer-paper templates on top. The piece is hand quilted with cotton thread. A tiny piping inside the binding accentuates the quilt. IDLEWOOD ROSE was awarded multiple first- and second-place ribbons.

June Kempston

IDLEWOOD ROSE

17" x 17"

Diane Lane

ARTIST'S STATEMENT

Having no official art training, I do not consider myself an artist, just a person who loves fabric and enjoys the relaxation of hand work. I love making miniature quilts because they are less time consuming yet still a way to create without so much of the tedious hand basting and quilting. Since I am not an outdoor gardener, quilts are the way I plant and compose my gardens. They will never wilt and perish.

BIO

Diane Lane has been making traditional quilts for almost forty years. The first workshops she took were in the early 1980s with Chris Wolf Edmonds and Jinny Beyer. It was in 1983 that Diane made her first miniature. She began competitive quilting in 1980 at the county fair level, and since then, her quilts have been the recipients of four AQS awards, six NQA awards, and two IQA awards. Several books and magazine publications have featured Diane's miniature quilts.

> QUILT DESCRIPTION

YELLOWLICIOUS is an original design that is styled after the antique Baltimore Album quilts. The corner heart blocks were inspired by Irma Gail Hatcher's book *Hearts*. This miniature is one in a series of traditional appliquéd quilts using just five floral-style templates. The texture was achieved by arranging diverse fragments of fabrics. Hand stitching highlights this small quilt.

YELLOWLICIOUS
18½" x 18½"

Suzanne Marshall

ARTIST'S STATEMENT

I have been making quilts for many years, but HOME SWEET HOME was the first miniature I had ever attempted. It gave me great pleasure to work with the small scraps from other quilts I had made and end up with a finished project. My little quilt won first prize in the miniature category at the Quintessential Quilt Exhibit in St. Louis, Missouri. Since most of my quilts are appliquéd and hand quilted, I was shocked and overjoyed. I smiled at Bill Schroeder's statement about my first miniature: "Not in a million years would I have guessed that this was a Suzanne Marshall quilt."

BIO

A self-taught quilter, Suzanne Marshall learned the art by trial and error. In 1988, she began entering competitions to receive critiques from the judges about her work. The first quilt she entered won a first-prize ribbon. Since then, her creations have received six prizes at the AQS Quilt Show and Contest (including two Best Hand Workmanship awards), the Grand Prize in Appliqué from Better Homes and Gardens, the Silver Award at Fabric Gardens, and several awards at the International Quilt Festival. Suzanne had the honor of being included in the top Thirty Distinguished Quiltmakers of the World exhibit in Tokyo, Japan, and has two quilts as part of the permanent collection in the Museum of the American Quilter's Society.

> QUILT DESCRIPTION

HOME SWEET HOME was inspired by the process used in Gwen Marston's *Liberated Quiltmaking*. All of the houses were made without the use of templates or knowing what they would look like before they were completed. The miniature is machine quilted.

HOME SWEET HOME
15½" x 18½"

Marie Moore

ARTIST'S STATEMENT

Romantica, by Patricia Campbell and Mimi Ayers, was the inspiration for this miniature. I scaled down the pattern for MIDSUMMER NIGHT. Working on the appliquéd flowers was such a joy, but quilting the dark navy background was a nightmare! Of the many miniatures I have created and showcased throughout the years, this one remains my favorite.

BIO

Although she always knew she had a passion for quilts and loved viewing them, it wasn't until 25 years ago that Marie Moore began quilting. At first, she worked with large quilts and a few baby quilts for friends, but it didn't take long before she knew her real passion in quiltmaking was in miniatures. Awards for her miniature work come from AQS, IQA, and Miniatures from the Heart.

> QUILT DESCRIPTION

MIDSUMMER NIGHT features brightly colored flowers on a dark navy background. The flowers, leaves, and stems are hand appliquéd with silk thread using the freezer-paper method. It is hand quilted with trapunto and embellished with embroidery

MIDSUMMER NIGHT

18" x 21"

Scott Murkin

ARTIST'S STATEMENT

Taking my cue from the layered structure of the quilt that has become my chosen medium of artistic expression, much of my work has to do with layers, both literal and figurative. Layers of color, light, and pattern. Layers of meaning. Layers of materials. Layers that occur in nature and those created by the hand of man and then added to and altered by the passage of time, the layer working in the fourth dimension. My most successful works combine a vivid image when viewed from several feet away with extra rewards for the viewer who takes the time to move in and examine them more closely.

BIO

A family practice and occupational medicine specialist, Scott Murkin, M.D., is originally from a large quilting family. Scott is an NQA certified quilt judge and enjoys doing programs and workshops for guilds, festivals, and quilt shops. Exhibited nationally and internationally, his quilts have appeared in numerous publications. He currently designs original quilts for the bed and wall.

> QUILT DESCRIPTION

BUTTERFLY FANDANGO was made for the 2004 Hoffman Challenge and was awarded second prize in the pieced division. It also won first place in the miniature category in the Randolph Quilter's Show in 2005. It is machine paper-foundation pieced and machine quilted. The inspiration for this quilt came from the traditional Pine Burr block.

Scott Murkin

BUTTERFLY FANDANGO

19½" x 19½"

Scott Murkin

> ## Quilt Description

SNAIL'S LAMÉ is machine paper-foundation pieced, machine quilted, and constructed entirely of cotton lamé fabrics. This gives the traditional Snail's Trail block a whole new twist. SNAIL'S LAMÉ was originally published in *A Few of My Favorite Miniature Quilts* by Christiane Meuniere. It received a first-place ribbon in the miniature category at the Old Church Gallery Quilter's Show in 2005.

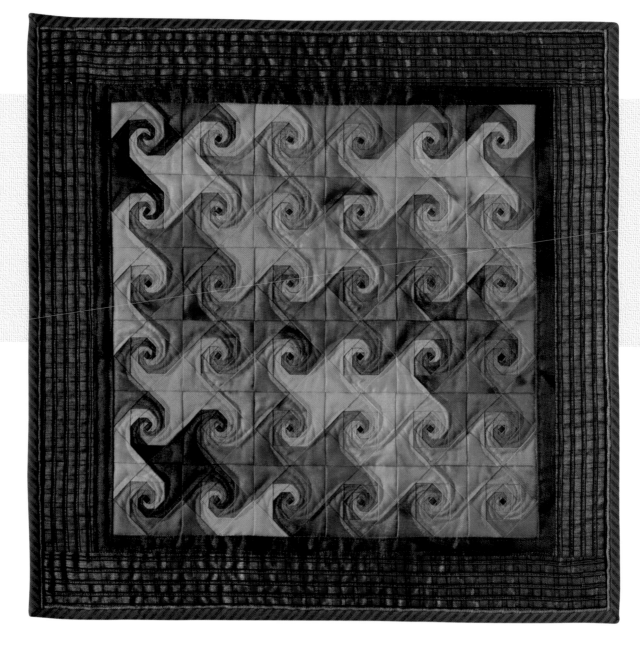

SNAIL'S LAMÉ

16½" x 16¼"

Sharon Norbutas

ARTIST'S STATEMENT

For centuries, bias has been used to enhance cling, drape, and flow in garments. The elegance of cowl necklines and the float of Ginger Rogers' skirts have always amazed me. Contemporary designers continue to find uses for bias in virtually every trend—from spaghetti straps to ruffles and turbans to evening gowns. I set out to find some way to include this technique in a quilt. The possibilities were endless. Bending bias, while tedious and time consuming, is a pleasure to me. I always end with yet another question in mind and another path to pursue.

BIO

Sharon Norbutas began quilting and quiltmaking over thirty years ago with a background in textiles and clothing. Teaching clothing construction at a local college is where her interest in quilting materialized. She was perplexed that all the quilt-related books available at that time ended the same way—"now quilt the top." After ordering a quilt frame from the Sears catalog, Sharon became entranced by quilting in every form. The last half of her quilting career, she pursued a specific interest in the use of bias. One of her many bias quilts has been designated a Masterpiece Quilt by NQA. She has been featured in several books and magazine articles, and has appeared on *Simply Quilts*.

> QUILT DESCRIPTION

BIAS MINIATURE 1 was produced as an experiment to find out how small bias curves can be and still create a successful piece. The miniature is made of 64 different blocks with 48 of them containing fourteen strips and the other sixteen containing eleven strips. It was made primarily with Daiwabo taupe fabrics that are representative of Japanese fabrics of the 1870s.

Sharon Norbutas

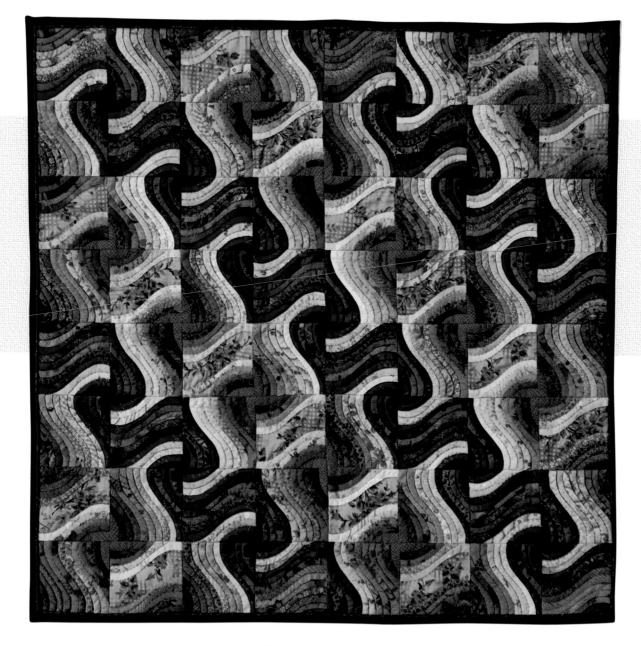

BIAS MINIATURE 1

20" x 20"

Lorraine Olsen

ARTIST'S STATEMENT

Figuring out how to reproduce this favorite pattern in miniature was exciting. Vintage Wedding Ring quilts inspired the trapunto, the narrow-shaped binding, and the scrap look. The details make it a best quilt to pack away and take out for special occasions. Old quilts tell a story with stains, worn bindings, and faded scraps saved from dresses, aprons, and baby clothes. My history, my love of fabric, and my heritage of master craftswomen is the story my quilt tells.

BIO

Using a square cardboard template, Lorraine Olsen made her first little quilt at the age of nine. Disappointed that the corners didn't match as she felt they should, her passion for quilting and technique was fueled. Quilting throughout her teenage years and into adulthood, she continued to fall in love with quilting. Miniature quiltmaking is what she finds most enjoyable, but the practical side of her gives her a longing to make baby quilts for the hospital and quick quilts to warm her family.

> QUILT DESCRIPTION

DOUBLE WEDDING RING was inspired by many vintage Double Wedding Ring quilts from books and collections. The pattern was adapted from *Folk Quilts and How to Recreate Them* by Audrey and Douglas Wiss. It was constructed using machine piecing, paper piecing, and hand appliqué. Hand quilting finishes this miniature.

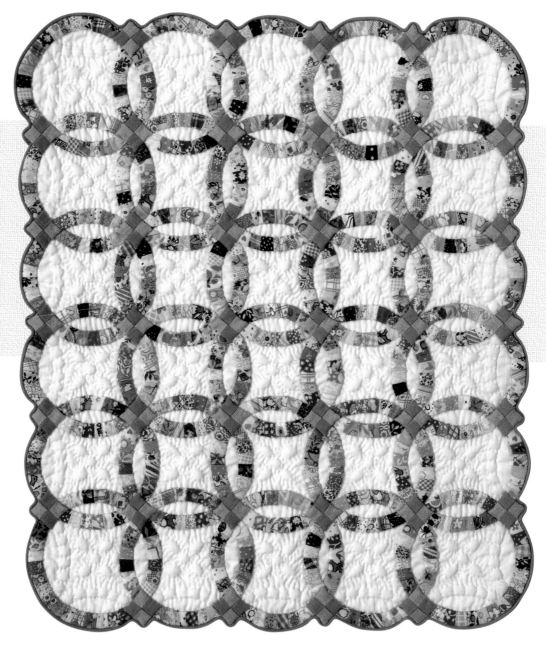

DOUBLE WEDDING RING

10¼" x 12"

Linda Roy

ARTIST'S STATEMENT

I do not have a formal art background but enjoy working with color and simple techniques. I frequently preassemble components to support my appliqué arrangements. In general, there are no deep rooted or profound messages in my designs, simply a desire to create something with my hands that is visually pleasing to myself. Making this little piece has sparked my interest in miniatures as well as teaching me how to improve overall scale and design. Quilting is a continual learning process, never ending.

BIO

Linda Roy had her first introduction to quiltmaking in 1989. Since then, designing traditional quilts and using handwork techniques have given her life a new enthusiasm. A hand quilter, her work has won numerous awards. She is a seven-time award winner at the AQS Quilt Show and Contest including the Best of Show purchase prize in 2005. In 2006, Linda's quilts won two Best of Show awards, one Best in World award, and a second place in the miniature category at the Asheville, North Carolina, show.

> QUILT DESCRIPTION

Although she is known for her colorful quilts, Linda made this white-on-white quilt so fading would never be a concern. ANTIQUE BISQUE showcases the simple elements such as bias bars, ruching, Cathedral Window strips, and stipple quilting that many of Linda Roy's large quilts acquire.

ANTIQUE BISQUE

19½" x 19½"

Anita Shackelford

ARTIST'S STATEMENT

The inspiration for this little quilt came from early French textiles. I love the texture of those wholecloth pieces, which were quilted in a combination of geometric design and floral or feather patterns, and often stuffed for more dramatic effect. I had explored raised work in several of my larger quilts and also in some garments and thought I wanted to try to capture the same texture and detail in a tiny quilt. Although the effect is subtle, I used padded trapunto for flower petals, corded channels as flower stems and an inner frame, stuffed work in the flower centers, and a variety of embroidery stitches for the finest details.

BIO

An internationally recognized teacher and lecturer, Anita Shackelford enjoys combining appliqué and fine hand quilting to create new quilts in the nineteenth-century style. A quiltmaker since 1967, Anita began teaching her art in 1980. She has been featured on popular television programs and in magazines. Her quilts have been exhibited in shows across the United States, in Australia, and in Japan. Her numerous award winners include 12 Best in Shows. A quilt judge, Anita serves on the faculty for NQA's Quilt Judging Seminar.

> QUILT DESCRIPTION

MINIATURE MARSEILLES is a miniature version of the all-white quilts made in eighteenth-century Marseilles, France. This miniature features a simple diamond grid quilting in the center and an elaborate floral design in the border. Border motifs are raised and embellished with cording, padding, stuffed work, and embroidery.

MINIATURE MARSEILLES

13" x 17½"

Nancy Ann Sobel

ARTIST'S STATEMENT

Making miniature quilts goes along with my fascination for tiny things—dolls, dollhouses, bottles, purses, glass, beadwork, etc. My miniature MIDWINTER NIGHT'S DREAM was a challenge to myself to miniaturize one of my larger quilts. What a wonderful and encouraging project it turned out to be! I embrace a simple creative lifestyle with my emphasis on my faith in God, family, home, and the appreciation of the beauty of the small things—like the tiny details in a flower petal. I owe my success in quilting to my grandma's encouragement to always do my best.

BIO

Nancy Ann Sobel learned to hand sew at the early age of four from her grandmother. Sewing was always a creative outlet for Nancy, as she graduated from doll clothes to making clothes for herself. It wasn't until forty years later that she decided to make quilts. Over the past twenty-five years, her quilts have won numerous awards and have been included in different publications.

> QUILT DESCRIPTION

A MIDWINTER NIGHT'S DREAM is an adaptation of the original full-size MIDWINTER NIGHT'S DREAM that won the Best Workmanship award in the 1990 AQS Quilt Show and Contest. Hand-embroidery around the snowflakes adds sparkle to the miniature. This piece was machine pieced, hand appliquéd, and hand quilted.

A MIDWINTER NIGHT'S DREAM

17½" x 17½"

Nancy Ann Sobel

> QUILT DESCRIPTION

KAUAI BLOSSOMS is an original Hawaiian quilt.
It is based on a pattern for a Hawaiian pillow.
Polyester batting, cotton fabric and thread, and
embroidery floss were used throughout this
hand-pieced, hand-appliquéd, hand-embroidered,
and hand-quilted miniature.

KAUAI BLOSSOMS

18¾" x 18¾"

Judy Spiers

ARTIST'S STATEMENT

I have worked with and enjoyed fabrics for a very long time, which has allowed quilting to become a natural extension of myself. Coming from a long line of quilters has helped me to appreciate just how far quilting has come in my lifetime. I have always felt the need to be creative, both physically and mentally. Quilting satisfies those needs and offers challenges that allow me to express my ideas, emotions, and feelings through my favorite mediums, fabric and thread. Quilting is a large part of who I am.

BIO

Despite enjoying sewing for most of her adult life and becoming an accomplished seamstress by the age of 18, it wasn't until 1996 that Judy Spiers discovered her interest in quilting. From there, she began researching patterns and methods of putting them together, took an appliqué class, and joined a local quilt guild. Her quilts have won numerous awards including two Best of Shows, three Viewer's Choice, one Judge's Choice, and several first-, second-, and third-place ribbons. Judy has been published in several magazine and newspaper articles.

> QUILT DESCRIPTION

PINEAPPLE FLAMBÉ was inspired by Jane Hall's beautiful Pineapple quilts. Using a computer program, the Pineapple block was designed with 77 pieces and then colored and arranged into a quilt. The quilt was foundation pieced using a lightweight interfacing material. Machine quilting with YLI thread finished this miniature.

PINEAPPLE FLAMBÉ

17" x 19"

Judy Spiers

> QUILT DESCRIPTION

PINEAPPLE SURPRISE is an original design Pineapple block pattern set in a Broken Star layout. Each of the blocks was machine pieced using a foundation made with featherweight interfacing and sewn together by hand. The miniature consists of seventy-seven pieces in each block, totaling 6,580 pieces in the quilt. Machine quilting enhances the design.

PINEAPPLE SURPRISE

20" x 20"

Patricia L. Styring

ARTIST'S STATEMENT

It has always been important for me to be original in quilts. I love curves and circles as they appear in all my work. I also see beauty in prairie points. Free-motion quilting gives me hours of joy as I am able to lose myself in the process. Quilting in miniature allows me to take on a challenge, yet finish before becoming overwhelmed. This quilt was made for the pure enjoyment of seeing how small I could work and still get sharp points.

BIO

As a way to be more expressive while sewing, Patricia Styring began the art of quiltmaking and quickly decided to enter competitions. Her quilts have been awarded ribbons six different times at the AQS Quilt Show and Contest, recognized with many other regional and national awards, and published in books, numerous magazines, and quilt calendars. Patricia also has a quilt in the permanent collection of the Museum of the American Quilter's Society.

> QUILT DESCRIPTION

MARINER'S QUILTEENIE is an original composition of four Mariner's Compasses adhering closely to a traditional appearance. The four-inch compass designs are surrounded by borders and generous free-form quilting. A tiny appliqué vine surrounds the center. The red-violet fabric, as well as the back of the quilt, was hand-dyed.

MARINER'S QUILTEENIE

13½" x 13½"

Myrl Lehman Tapungot & Friends

ARTIST'S STATEMENT

Some of our quilts can easily take over a year of dedicated effort to complete. We pride ourselves in making quilts with near perfect, identical stitches, and even experts using magnifying glasses find it difficult or impossible to tell the difference. Our "single stab stitch" method gives the appearance of uniformity that is unparalleled in the quilting industry.

*Note: The Artist statement was taken from Myrl's Web site — www.mdeans.com

BIO

A competitive quiltmaker and resident of the Philippines, Myrl Tapungot enjoys working with others to create quilts to enter into contests. Her quilts feature all handwork and are entered in international shows. In 1997, she was the recipient of the Gingher Hand Workmanship Award at the AQS Quilt Show and Contest. Myrl's group quilts have received numerous ribbons.

> QUILT DESCRIPTION

LE JARDIN DE NOS RÊVES SAMPLER was based on Myrl's orginal design award-winning quilt of the same name. It was inspired by vintage molded ceiling designs. The trapunto areas were "stab stitch" quilted with colored thread through the quilt top and a second layer of muslin. Colored yarns were stuffed in the trapunto areas to add subtle shading. This miniature is entirely hand quilted.

LE JARDIN DE NOS RÊVES SAMPLER

8¾" x 10¼"

Alice Tignor

ARTIST'S STATEMENT

I love the experience of selecting, cutting, and shaping fine fabric into wonderful miniature designs and physical shapes. My technique engages vintage fabric, precision handwork, and playful inventiveness using traditional patterns. For me, quilting is the "cutting-edge" where passion and artistry live. Whether I am touched by the feel, sight, or smell of a new or old quilt, I know that it holds the heart of the maker in its threads and the life of the owner in its fabric.

BIO

Alice Tignor began her quiltmaking journey twenty-five years ago when she began reproducing vintage quilts. Gradually, she began making miniatures and entering them into competitions. Her quilts have won several awards at local and regional quilt shows. This miniature received a third-place ribbon in the miniature category at the 2005 Asheville, North Carolina, Quilt Show.

> QUILT DESCRIPTION

MY LITTLE MARINER'S COMPASS SAMPLER contains nine three-inch designs: Ohio Star, Log Cabin, Grandmother's Flower Garden, Bear's Paw, Mariner's Compass, Churn Dash, Tumbling Blocks, Dutchman's Puzzle, and Amish Star. The rich colors of Civil War fabrics integrate the various designs. Log Cabin corner blocks finish this hand-quilted miniature.

Alice Tignor

MY LITTLE MARINER'S COMPASS SAMPLER

15½" x 15½"

Elsie Vredenburg

ARTIST'S STATEMENT

I quilt because I love fabric in its many colors and patterns. I love cutting it up and sewing it back together to make new designs. Even though I always said I had no artistic talent and avoided art classes, I think deep in my heart, this is what I always longed to be able to do. I make quilts for enjoyment—both mine and others.

BIO

After receiving a bachelor of science degree in home economics education from Michigan State University, Elsie Vredenburg eventually decided to stay at home and allow quilting to take over. Currently, she is an active teacher, focusing mainly on freezer-paper piecing. Her quilts have allowed her to establish a line of wallhanging patterns that feature lighthouses. When she is not on the road teaching, Elsie likes to complete one to two quilts for exhibit each year.

QUILT DESCRIPTION

AMISH EASTER BASKETS REVISITED was inspired by Elsie's award-winning large quilt AMISH EASTER BASKETS that is now a part of the permanent collection of the Museum of the American Quilter's Society. Updated with hand-dyed fabric and machine quilting, this miniature features four Cake Stand blocks set with sashing to form a cross. It was machine pieced, with a hand-appliquéd triangle border.

AMISH EASTER BASKETS REVISITED

22½" x 22½"

Debra Wagner

ARTIST'S STATEMENT

I have never made a quilt, even a full-size one, that has had as many major mishaps as this miniature. I thought more than once about not finishing it. But because of all its mistakes, it is special to me. I learned so much about patience, humor, luck, humility, and maybe even a bit about miracles. It was a miracle that all 2,300 pieces fit together and that the finished quilt was square. Even through all the trials, I learned so many great lessons and stand amazed that I finished this miniature.

BIO

Debra Wagner began sewing at the age of nine when her parents became sewing machine dealers. She received her degree in clothing textiles and design, specializing in lace and traditional textile methods. It was in the 1980s that she began the art of machine quilting. Two of her quilts have received the AQS Machine Workmanship Award. RAIL THROUGH THE ROCKIES was designated a Master Quilt and chosen as one of the top 100 quilts of the 20th century. An author of four quilting books and quiltmaking teacher for several years, Debra retired from quilting in 2000 to work in the family sewing machine dealership.

QUILT DESCRIPTION

COULD N' WOULD was inspired by an antique quilt in a photograph. It was entirely machine quilted and machine pieced using the traditional method. This miniature was made for the sole purpose of the Oh, Wow! collection.

COULD N' WOULD

22" x 22"

Trudy Søndrol Wasson

ARTIST'S STATEMENT

Since I was a little girl, I have always loved working with fabric and the sewing machine. I have been a Norwegian rosemaler for over thirty years. The flow of the quilting design is very important to me and it is easy to see how my painting influences my quilting designs. I enjoy taking my painting designs and making them into small quilts. My future goal is to design larger pieces using a combination of appliqué and "rosemaling" machine quilting.

BIO

At the early age of seventeen, Trudy Søndrol Wasson was using her knowledge of the sewing machine to make garments. She took home a first-place ribbon in the local and regional Singer Sewing Contest and an honorable mention at the national contest that followed. However, it wasn't until several years later that Trudy developed her enthusiasm for quiltmaking. Her first quilt was a baby quilt for her grandson and her interest grew from there. In both 2005 and 2006 Trudy had miniature quilts juried into the AQS Quilt Show and Contest.

> QUILT DESCRIPTION

HEARTS A-PLENTY was created using a heart inside a heart design accented with feather quilting. Echo stitching and small stippling fill the background. Hand-dyed cotton sateen fabric was used with wool batting and silk thread to add luster to the quilting.

HEARTS A-PLENTY

23" x 23"

Mariya Waters

ARTIST'S STATEMENT

Miniature quilts are a wonderful art form that allows a large-scale design to be reduced to a snapshot. Artistic and workmanship skills can be tested to their limit to produce a wonderful piece of work that is as easy to hang as any piece of art. Many of my quilts, including ENIGMA 3, have been inspired by antique ceiling panels. I am proud that through seeing my work, other people are inspired to work towards improving their quilting skills.

BIO

Mariya Waters is an international award-winning quiltmaker and teacher. Her specialties include hand appliqué, machine trapunto, machine quilting, and miniature quilts. Mariya began quilting in 1990 and four years later won her first major quilting award in England. Since then, all of her major quilts have won both local and international awards. Many of her works have appeared in books, magazines, and advertisements; others have been acquired for either public or private collections. Quilting and teaching others the art have turned into her full-time job.

> QUILT DESCRIPTION

ENIGMA 3 is a quilt in a series of limited edition wholecloth quilts made using pink Thai silk satin. The inspiration for this quilt came from pressed metal ceilings from the Victorian era and also the beautiful seventeenth-century plaster ceilings in European buildings. This quilt took three days to draw and sixty hours to machine quilt using rayon thread.

ENIGMA 3
15¾" x 15¾"

Deborah L. White

ARTIST'S STATEMENT

After making a scaled-down version of one of my larger quilts in response to my friend's desire, I fell in love with the intricacy of making miniatures. I immensely enjoy the detailed handwork in the small quilts. Even in a miniature, I approach border designs with as much importance as the body of the quilt. Also in this vein, I have always viewed the quilting design as the breath of life of the quilt.

BIO

Finding her creativity at an early age, Deborah White has since become an accomplished quiltmaker and author. It was in 1982 that she took her first quilting lessons at a local library. She began entering local, regional, and national contests and has won numerous awards at all levels. Her OAK LEAF WITH CHERRIES miniature quilt received three first-place ribbons and one second-place ribbon.

> QUILT DESCRIPTION

OAK LEAF WITH CHERRIES was inspired by the falling leaves of the autumn season. After designing the quilt with an oak leaf theme and enhancing it with cherries, frayed pieces of fabric were soaked in Fray Check™ and formed like a yo-yo. The border and quilting designs were chosen to enhance the simplicity of the blocks and tantalize the eyes throughout.

OAK LEAF WITH CHERRIES

15" x 15"

Deborah L. White

> QUILT DESCRIPTION

LA FLEUR D'ABEILLE was created on the inspiration of making a namesake quilt. Designed on a computer, this miniature showcases the combination of the Honey Bee block and a primitive interpretation of the bee balm flower. The borders encompass the design as in a formal garden. The bees are silk-ribbon embroidered and the entire quilt has additional embroidered enhancements.

Deborah L. White

LA FLEUR D'ABEILLE

17" x 17"

Yo Yo Club of Paducah

ARTIST'S STATEMENT

Volunteering at the quilt museum has been a blessing to all of us. We greatly enjoy working with the visitors. However, our mission is to help those organizations that are in the process of helping individuals and families in unfortunate circumstances. The gratification and blessings received far outweigh the time and effort spent in this work.

BIO

The Yo Yo Club of Paducah was founded in 1998 when the Museum of the American Quilter's Society asked a small group of volunteers to demonstrate making yo-yos at various activities. This group of five women now quilts in the lobby of the museum once a week and helps in many areas. The "Yo-Yos"—Charlotte Roberts, Anita Manning, Carolyn Carver, Virginia Hancock, and Pat Lewis—also make and sell baby quilts, cards, and Christmas ornaments using the proceeds to benefit local charities. They have been featured in different magazine and newspaper articles.

> QUILT DESCRIPTION

YO YO BASKET OF FLOWERS was created using 1930s' reproduction fabrics. The yo-yos were made by all five members of the group and sewn together into the basket and flowers. After the base was completed, the basket with the flowers was appliquéd. The piece was hand quilted by Pat Lewis.

YO YO BASKET OF FLOWERS

10" x 12"

Cross Reference

QUILTS